WAGS & WHIMSY

Truffle, Adam & The Magical Bone

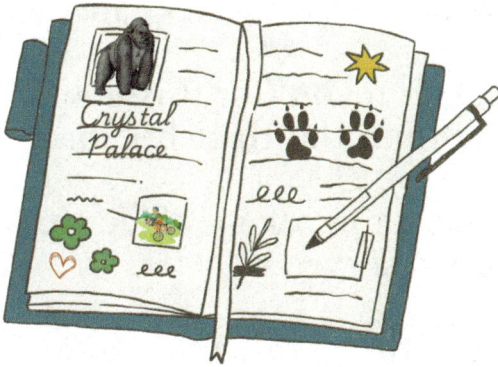

by Agnieszka Gradzewicz-Akal

Illustrated by Dan Tama

COPYRIGHTS

First published in Great Britain on 30th October 2024 by Agnieszka Gradzewicz-Akal

ISBN: 978-1-0687281-0-5 - Paperback

www.TruffleAndAdam.com

Written by Agnieszka Gradzewicz-Akal
Edited by Tom McBrien
Cover and Illustrations Design by Dan Tama

A catalogue record for this book is available from the British Library.

DEDICATION

To my little pack, that I love more
and more every day.
A

CONTENTS

Chapter 1: **Magic in Crystal Palace Park**   **3**

Chapter 2: **Whispers of the Mysterious Stranger**   **19**

Chapter 3: **Into the Maze**   **36**

Chapter 4: **Quest for the Mysterious Artefact** **49**

Chapter 5: **A Hero's Flight**   **59**

Chapter 6: **Dancing in the Air**   **77**

PROLOGUE

WOOF! ARF! BARK!

"Allow me to introduce myself. I'm Truffle, and I'm a one-of-a-kind sausage dog – half dachshund, half pure magic. I come from Poland, the land of pierogies and sausages. I now live in London with my wonderful human parents, Aga and Matt, and my best pal, Adam. Oh, and I can't forget my loyal canine friend, Olly.

We three go on the most amazing adventures together. This is the story of our most recent one – the mystery of the magical bone! Settle into your seat and join me on a thrilling journey of mystery and magic through the enchanted Crystal Palace Park – and maybe a few sausages too! Are you ready to dive in? Let's go before Olly eats all the snacks!"

CHAPTER 1:

MAGIC IN CRYSTAL PALACE PARK

The door swung open and Adam's voice rang out full of challenge and cheer. "Truffle! Race you to the bike rack. Last one there is a rotten egg!" he shouted, darting out the door with a grin.

Adam was my little brother, my sidekick, and my best friend. His brown hair and dark eyes were a mirror of mine.

"Challenge accepted!" I answered with a happy bark, sprinting after him, my long ears flapping wildly as I raced along. I reached the bike rack first, with Adam arriving seconds after me, panting and laughing.

"Almost got you that time, Truffle!" he exclaimed, bending down to ruffle my fur. "One of these days I'll beat you to the finish line!"

Aga and Matt, our parents, caught up to us.

Aga, with her hair in a ponytail and a smile playing on her lips, said warmly, "You two are quite the pair."

"It's the first day of school holidays! Let's get on the bikes. We'll cycle to Crystal Palace Park," Matt prompted us.

"Yes!" Adam exclaimed. He pulled a small notebook from his pocket. "I want to find something new for my guidebook today.

There are still so many parts of the park we haven't discovered yet. We will explore everything so much faster with our bikes!"

I wagged my tail enthusiastically, along happily beside my adopted family. My long, awkward legs (well, long for a dachshund!) had a mind of their own.

They carried me through the lush greenery. It was so different from the snowy fields of my Polish homeland.

The park was alive with the morning's magic signalling the glorious beginning of the summer holidays. Ducks glided on the lake, squirrels scampered up the oaks, and the sweet scent of blooming flowers mingled with earthy dampness.

I dashed through the greenery, my nose twitching at all the new scents. Ahead, the park's towering dinosaur statues loomed through the mist as if they were having tea with the Egyptian Sphinx.

As we neared the terraced area of the park, I spotted Olly, my canine companion and park buddy. His tail wagged in anticipation. Olly was older and wiser and had fur as dark as midnight. I barked excitedly, my paws dancing on the path. Adam slowed down and waited for me to leap gracefully into his bike's front basket.

"Hey, Olly, hop into the trailer!" Adam called out cheerfully.

With a joyful bark, Olly bounded into the small trailer attached to the back of Adam's bike and together we set off again, the breeze ruffling our fur as we sped along the winding paths.

"Eio, little bunch! Slow down!" Aga called out, laughing. Her voice, with its familiar Polish accent, was always a comfort to me. It reminded me of home, of pierogies and playful days with my siblings Peanut, Coco, Buli, and Oreo. I missed them and our chaotic games, but here, today, in this magical new world, I felt joyful.

6

Matt, who was always the planner, carried a backpack filled with treats and a frisbee, ready for any adventure.

Adam stopped the bike and with a notebook in one hand and a pencil in the other, began documenting every little bug, bird, and tree that we had passed.

His curiosity about the natural world matched my own, though mine was more about scents and sounds than sketches and notes.

"What are you writing?" I barked curiously.

Adam looked up with a shy but proud smile. "I'm updating my guidebook of the park," he explained. "I want to document every tree and bird that lives here. Maybe I'll discover a new species! There's so much to explore."

His enthusiasm was infectious and I soon found myself eagerly sniffing around, hoping to uncover something new for his guidebook.

Today was more than just a walk in the park. It was an exploration, a shared adventure.

"You know, Adam," I began, "I used to race my brother Peanut back in Poland. Whoever came last was a slobbery doggy toy!" I let out a joyful bark, remembering how our laughter echoed through the fields.

"One time, we thought we discovered a new species. It was small, furry, and moved in the funniest way. We barked for everyone to come see. It turned out it was just a hedgehog rolled up in a ball! We felt so silly, but we laughed about it for days!"

Adam burst out laughing. "A hedgehog! That's hilarious, Truffle. I guess not every discovery is a new species, but it's always fun to explore."

Thinking about those playful times with my siblings, I continued, "I loved those days in Poland with my family. We had so much

fun together. But one day, while we were playing, some scary humans showed up.

Their faces were so twisted they looked like pretzels! They scooped us all up – me, Peanut, Coco, Buli, and Oreo – and stuffed us into a clunky, cramped van that smelled like old sausages.

It was the bumpiest ride ever, and we had no idea where they were taking us."

I paused, then added with a playful grin, "But hey, at least we had each other, even if the van smelled like a sausage factory. I thought I might turn into a sausage with all that smell!"

"Sounds like you traded one wild ride for another, Truffle," Adam gently smiled.

"Exactly!" I wagged my tail enthusiastically. "Instead of worrying about twisted pretzel faces, now we worry about solving mysteries and searching for treasures."

Adam stood up. "Truffle! Look, I see something over there. Maybe it's a new species. Or a treasure! Come, let's find out."

Olly, who had been busy quietly observing a playful squirrel, looked up. "Speaking of treasures, Adam," Olly interjected, "Did you know this park is rumoured to have a secret treasure of its own?"

"A real treasure?" Adam's eyes widened in amazement.

"It's an old park legend," Olly said with a twinkle in his eye. "No one knows exactly where it is, but they say it's been hidden here for centuries."

"I believe it! I can feel something in the air, almost like there's magic in the breeze."

I lifted my head and sniffed curiously. "Where is it coming from? Can we find it?"

I barked excitedly, intrigued. I felt the tingling feeling in my paws too, and it was growing stronger. It wasn't just the thrill of the hunt.

It felt like the echo of a deeper magic. A special kind of magic that brought excitement to the air.

Adam clapped his hands together. "Let's go look for it! What if it's buried right under our noses?"

We immediately embarked on our impromptu treasure hunt. Olly sniffed the air thoughtfully. "This park is full of wonders. Maybe you're sensing the magic that's said to be hidden here."

A little while later, Adam knelt down beside me. "I heard mysterious sounds around the park today. Do you think it's a clue to the treasure?"

"It could be," I replied. "Maybe the treasure isn't gold or jewels. Maybe it's something even more special."

We continued our exploration, Adam jotting down notes and sketches while I sniffed out potential clues. We soon stumbled upon our first clue, a peculiar-looking tree with strange markings.

Adam examined it closely and added it to his guidebook, noting it as a potential lead. The thrill of discovering something new made our hearts race.

"Look at this, Truffle!" Adam gasped, pointing to a spot near the base of a tree where an old, rusty key was partially buried in the dirt.

I barked in excitement. "Do you think it's a clue?"

Adam kneeled down and carefully dug out the key. "It must be! This is turning out to be the best summer holiday ever!"

Olly wagged his tail. "This park is full of surprises. Who knows what we'll find next?"

Adam put the key in his pocket and we resumed our search for clues. I soon noticed something peculiar on the floor: a series of small, round footprints that didn't belong to any animal I knew. I barked and Adam and Olly came to take a look.

Adam examined the footprints and frowned. He quickly drew the shape into his guidebook. "These are strange. They don't look like they belong to any animal I've seen before."

Olly sniffed the tracks, his ears perking up. "I've heard whispering among the local animals about a mysterious stranger wandering the park. Maybe these footprints are connected."

"A mysterious stranger? Do you think they could be after the treasure too?"

Adam's eyes sparkled with excitement. "It's possible! But there are lots of strange people in the park. We should follow these tracks and see where they lead. This could be a big clue!"

We followed the footprints deeper into Crystal Palace Park, towards where the dinosaur statues stood tall. I could feel the sense of adventure grow stronger. The park seemed to buzz with the promise of hidden wonders and magical secrets.

We knew that this was just the beginning of something extraordinary. With each step, we were closer to uncovering the mysteries of strange footprints.

But before we could trace them to their source, Matt's voice rang out. "Adam! Truffle! Olly! It's time to go!"

We quickly packed up our things and made our way home. Olly was coming to our home for a sleepover. The summer holidays were off to an incredible start, and we were all buzzing with excitement, dreaming of uncovering every mystery Crystal Palace Park had to offer.

After a hearty dinner, a sense of contentment settled over us.

But as the evening settled and shadows stretched across the park, the laughter of the day faded into the quiet of night, and a subtle unease began to stir in the air. "Something feels different tonight," I murmured, falling asleep.

CHAPTER 2:

WHISPERS OF THE MYSTERIOUS STRANGER

Over the next few days following our treasure hunt, Adam, Olly, and I noticed subtle, strange occurrences around the park. It began with the ducks.

Normally chatty and carefree, they huddled together, whispering in hushed tones. When I asked what was wrong, they only quacked nervously about missing breadcrumbs.

Next, the squirrels, always the gossipers of the park, began to chatter about shadows moving in the twilight. "More rats than usual," they squeaked, their tails twitching with anxiety.

Adam was immediately intrigued. "Truffle, Olly, something strange is happening. It must be connected to the treasure," he said, pulling out his guidebook.

Adam meticulously recorded everything about the park, and these strange events were no exception.

We decided to investigate, turning our regular playful romps into careful patrols. On one such afternoon patrol, we finally saw him – a figure shrouded in a cloak, moving stealthily near the old oak tree. He stood by the duck pond but didn't feed the ducks, which was very suspicious.

"Look, Adam," I whispered. "There's someone by the pond. And he's not even feeding the ducks! What's he doing there?"

Adam's quickly jotted down notes in

his guidebook. "You're right, that *is* strange. We have to do something about it, Truffle. Maybe he's searching for the treasure too."

My nose twitched with suspicion. "Yes. We need to keep an eye on him," I whispered.

With Adam's encouragement and a looming sense of adventure hanging over us, we devised a plan to observe the stranger and follow his shadowy actions.

Our mission was clear: uncover who this mysterious figure was and find out if he was after the treasure as well.

"The animals grew restless," I thought to myself. "The trees are whispering warnings, and the wind carries a scent of danger – or is that just Olly's breakfast?"

We kept a watchful eye on the mysterious stranger from a distance. He made his way through the park with a purpose, his steps measured and stealthy. Each secretive glance he cast and each odd pause he took only multiplied our questions.

Who was this cloaked figure? What was he searching for in our peaceful heaven?

The figure's presence marked a turning point in our search. His actions slowly began to make sense. It was clear that he was searching for something, probing the earth like a treasure hunter with a faulty metal detector with each step he took.

That afternoon, as the sun's glow stretched over Crystal Palace Park, we decided to take a little boat out on the lake to patrol the water before heading home for tea. Adam paddled while I perched at the bow, and Olly happily swam alongside us, his tail wagging as he splashed in the water.

"I bet I can swim faster than you can paddle, Adam," Olly barked playfully. "I'll race you to the statues!"

"Yeah, right, Olly! This is a race you won't win!" Adam laughed, putting more effort into his paddling.

We neared the statues. A gentle breeze carried a faint whisper to my ears, **"Truffle, Truffle…"** The soft, eerie voice seemed to drift on the wind itself.

"Who is whispering my name?" I perked up, my ears twitching and my fur bristling with unease.

Adam paused mid-paddle, his eyes wide as he looked around. "D-did you hear that too?" he asked, his voice shaking.

Olly stopped swimming and floated next to the boat, his ears perked up too. "I heard it! This is getting weird."

We scanned the dimming park from our boat. The whisper seemed to come from a grand statue of a dinosaur, which towered over the pond like a guardian of forgotten secrets. Its eyes, usually dull and lifeless in the last light of day, now seemed to flicker with hidden knowledge.

"Truffle, did you know there is an ancient artefact hidden in the park?" the dinosaur's voice suddenly boomed, resonating deep and clear, its stone mouth unmoving yet unmistakably the source.

"An old park legend says that it possesses a power that can be used for great good… or terrible evil. The mysterious stranger you follow seeks to harness it for darkness."

Adam's brow furrowed in confusion. "What's an artefact?" he asked, his voice a mixture of both fear and fascination.

"An artefact is like an old treasure, Adam," I explained, my mind racing with the gravity of our discovery. "It's a very old item, sometimes even magical, with powers beyond our understanding."

"Magic can be used for good or for bad." Adam's voice was nervous, yet his small hands clenched in determination.

"The question is, how do we stop the mysterious stranger?" he asked the dinosaur.

But the dinosaur had returned to its usual stone state, the magic of its speech having faded away as quickly as it had appeared.

"We must stop them, Truffle, Adam," Olly barked, paws splashing in the water.

"Yes," I agreed. My mind whirling with plans. "But let's skip the dressing up this time. Remember the time you dressed up with a moustache? You looked more like a walrus than a spy." Our spirits lifted slightly at the memory. A chuckle escaped my throat despite the seriousness of our situation. With a renewed sense of purpose, we prepared to confront the dangers ahead.

The park started to darken as nighttime neared. We could sense the shadowy figure lurking nearby. We could only hope he was unaware of our newfound knowledge.

★ ★ ★

We decided it was time to gather more information. "We need a full park assembly," Adam declared, his mind set on unravelling the mystery.

That evening, the park's residents assembled beneath the branches of the grand oak. The ducks waddled in first, quacking about the disruption to their peaceful pond-side routines.

"Ever since that shifty stranger showed up, our breadcrumbs have gone missing," quacked Daphne Duck, her feathers ruffled with annoyance. "Breadcrumbs don't just walk away by themselves, you know!"

"I've seen shadows – lots of them – slipping around after dark," squeaked Sarah Squirrel, her bushy tail twitching with every word. "It's not just us squirrels stashing extra nuts, I tell you!"

From the back, Larry Llama added with a dramatic flair, "And I've been hearing strange noises at night, like someone's whispering ancient spells. Or maybe they're just bad at singing. It's hard to tell."

"We need to find out who he is," I said, doing my best to keep the meeting focused amidst the chatter of worried wildlife.

Olly, channelling his inner detective, adjusted an imaginary cap. "Let's not leap into any ponds or, heavens forbid, fall out of any trees while we're at it. We need to be very careful," he quipped, earning a few nervous chuckles from the assembly.

Benny Badger, known for his gruff voice and blunt words, grunted, "I've sniffed around his footprints. Smells like trouble – and a bit like old cheese."

With each creature's report, the picture grew clearer and our concerns grew deeper. This wasn't just about missing breadcrumbs or spooky shadows. There was something bad a foot, and it was clear that it had something to do with the mysterious stranger.

"We'll need everyone's help to keep an eye on the stranger. The park, maybe even the whole of London, depends on it. Watch carefully, and stay safe," I instructed. I felt the weight of leadership on my shoulders.

"Anything for the park!" a tiny robin chirped from above, her voice bright and determined.

"Anything for the park!" the whole assembly repeated.

The air buzzed as creatures big and small pledged to protect our shared home. With humour to lift our spirits, determination to guide us, and a sprinkle of park magic to motivate us, we were ready to face whatever this mysterious stranger had planned.

Adam and I said our goodbyes to Olly and made our way home to where Aga was waiting for us. "Right on time. Dinner is ready," she announced with a warm smile.

Adam and I gathered around the table and eagerly recounted our day's adventures. "... And then the dinosaur statue talked to us!" Adam exclaimed, eyes wide with excitement.

Aga listened intently, then said, "I do feel magic and mystery in the air. The two of you and Olly are not just an ordinary team, you're the guardians of magic and the protectors of Crystal Palace Park."

I couldn't help but add while swallowing a mouthful of dinner, "And, of course, connoisseurs of fine sausage. Well, at least I am."

Everyone burst into laughter. Matt chuckled, "That's our Truffle. Always thinking about food!"

As we laughed and shared stories, I felt a warm sense of belonging. Our adventures were only just beginning, and with my family by my side, I knew that we could face anything that came our way.

CHAPTER 3:

INTO THE MAZE

The whispers about the artefact were so persistent that they'd become the talk of Crystal Palace Park and the nearby animal farm. It wasn't just chittering gossip. It was an urgent symphony of hooves, feathers, and whiskers. Adam, Olly, and I felt it. A weight as concerning to us as a squirrel caught without its stash in winter.

"How will we find the artefact before the mysterious stranger does?" I asked.

A serious look crossed Adam's face. "Don't worry, Truffle. You're great at sniffing out things, and Olly knows the park better than anyone. I can help with maps and history. We make a good team, don't we? We just need to make a plan."

I barked in agreement and Olly wagged his tail enthusiastically. Adam, who turns eight in a few months, was more than just our companion. He was a vital part of our team, bringing his unique strengths to our adventure.

"But finding things without clues is hard. It's not like these mystical objects come with GPS tags, do they?" Adam continued, looking perplexed.

Thus began our quest to find clues.

The park was full of strange and wonderful things. Not just the ponds and the green lawns, but also the perplexing dinosaur statues that played an eternal game of hide-and-seek with anyone who dared look their way. Even the stone Egyptian Sphinxes seemed to smirk knowingly as if in a joke we weren't privy to.

"The dinosaur said the artefact is old.

Let's head to the oldest part of the park and look around there," I suggested, eager to unravel the park's secrets.

Adam's eyes lit up. "That's near the Victorian section!" he smiled. "I read that the Victorians built that part of the park over a century ago and that it has some of the park's oldest trees. The Crystal Palace Maze is there too. It might hold clues about the magic here."

I wagged my tail, impressed. Adam's knack for history would come in handy on our quest.

We set off across the park, walking what felt like a million miles, each step slower than a sleepy tortoise.

★ ★ ★

We stood at the entrance to the maze. Olly looked around, his nose twitching with anticipation. "Alright, team. Are we ready for this?" he asked, trying to sound braver than he felt.

"Let's go find that artefact and save the world," Adam replied, clutching his notepad like a shield.

"Remember, eyes and ears open," I whispered. "Mazes are designed to trick us."

The moment we stepped into the maze, the atmosphere changed. The tall hedges rose up around us like ancient walls, their leaves rustling as if sharing age-old secrets.

We slowly walked through the green corridors. The first challenge appeared as soon as we reached a junction in the path.

A wise old owl perched on a long tree branch eyed us with a knowing look. "To advance, answer me this," the owl hooted solemnly. "What flies forever, yet rests nearly never?"

Adam scribbled in his notebook, muttering to himself. A moment later his eyes lit up. "The wind!" he exclaimed.

"Very astute, young one," the owl nodded, pointing a feathery wing deeper into the maze and showing us the way.

Next, a band of little foxes slinked from the underbrush. Their leader sported a slick grin. "Fancy a break from your quest?" he offered, waving a paw towards a small, neatly dug hole. "I have a luxurious den available for rent, complete with room service and soft moss bedding!"

"Uh, thanks, but we're kind of in the middle of something," I replied, nudging Adam and Olly to ignore them and continue forward.

The fox shrugged dramatically. "Your loss!

If you change your mind, we have a special on autumn leaves and a complimentary acorn collection!"

We continued deeper into the maze until the path opened into a small clearing with several paths. A tiny, surprisingly animated polar bear statue loomed before us. It was posed as if caught mid-stride, and its stone eyes gleamed with a playful light.

"It's not often I get visitors way out here," the polar bear boomed, its rumbling voice matching its icy visage. "Trying to navigate the maze, are you? I might just have a frosty tip for you."

Olly barked a laugh, unable to resist. "Did you just make a joke?"

"Perhaps," the polar bear winked, or at least it seemed to. "When you find yourself lost, follow the direction of the sun at noon. It'll lead you as straight as the North Star does at night."

Taking the bear's advice, we waited for the sun to reach its peak, then watched as its shadow pointed steadily down one of the paths in the clearing that had looked uncertain before.

As we followed the sun's shadow, a chorus of chirping crickets drew our attention to a hidden alcove. "Chirp twice, turn left, chirp once, go straight," they sang in unison.

"Sounds like a musical map," I mused. "Or they just are trying to distract us from our way. This seems way too convenient," Adam said with suspicion.

So we continued to navigate the winding paths, our steps tentative at first as we followed their tuneful instructions. The maze was a puzzle, its twisting turns and dead ends testing our limits.

All of a sudden, a loud rumbling noise echoed, startling us all. Olly and Adam turned to look at me with raised eyebrows. "Excuse me, just a bit peckish over here,"

I apologised with a sheepish grin. "I'm hoping we can tweak the artefact's power to turn sticks into sausages – or maybe even bacon!"

Olly chuckled and said, "That's got to be the mysterious stranger's secret weapon – using rumbling bellies to sabotage our mission!" Everyone burst into laughter.

We soon reached another junction and had to stop once again, unsure of which way to turn next. There were no statues or animals to guide us this time.

Just as we started to feel a bit lost, my stomach rumbled again, causing another round of giggles.

"Look, guys! Gold stones. They must be our guiding signs," Adam said, pointing to a series of small carved golden stones that dotted the path at various intervals. "We passed a few of them before." Adam bent down and traced his fingers over the intricate carvings. "Each one has a different emblem. There was an owl before, then a bear. Now it's a bee," he recited, his eyes wide with wonder. "They're telling us which way to go so we don't walk in circles!"

Olly sniffed the stone with the bee carved into it, then peered down the left path. "Bees are busy and purposeful, right? Maybe following the bee will lead us further through the maze," he suggested.

"Good thinking, Olly," Adam nodded. "Let's follow the bee path and see where it leads us."

Eager to uncover the next part of the maze and get closer to the hidden treasure, we set off down the path. Before long, we arrived at another clearing where the path suddenly diverged in several directions again, each marked by different emblems. We paused, unsure which to choose next.

"This must be a puzzle," Adam mused. "Each emblem must be telling us something about the direction they're pointed."

That's when I noticed a bush nearby rustling suspiciously. "Did you see that?" I whispered, my fur standing on edge.

Olly and Adam came closer, squinting at the bush. "Something's moving in there," Olly growled softly, his body tense.

Adam pinched his nose with his fingers and gasped, "Whatever it is, it smells like really old cheese."

Just then, a low voice drifted towards us from the rustling bush. "You think you can solve the secrets of the maze so easily?" The voice was mocking, chilling. We couldn't see the speaker, but the hidden threat was clear. The bush stopped rattling and the voice disappeared as fast as it first appeared.

Adam clutched my side, his bravery faltering slightly. "What do we do now, Truffle? Which path should we take?"

I looked between the stones, each emblem seemingly alive in the sunlight. The decision weighed heavily on me, knowing that each choice would lead us closer to danger and to the artefact we had sworn to protect.

"We need to choose wisely," I whispered.

"My mum always says you have to follow your heart when making decisions," Adam suddenly piped up. "But in this case, follow your nose!"

"A nose?" Me and Olly asked, confused.

"Yes, Truffle! Sniff out the path for clues!" Adam almost yelled, laughing.

"That **is** what I am famous for," I chuckled as I leaned down to sniff out the route.

CHAPTER 4:

QUEST FOR THE MYSTERIOUS ARTEFACT

We advanced through the maze, navigating the way using the golden emblems. The paths were becoming increasingly tricky. We dodged animated rose bushes that hurled thorns at us like seasoned archers and pushed through thick bushes whose branches poked at our faces. It wasn't just physical. The air itself was thick with a mystical energy. It felt as if the park's magic was more concentrated here, swirling around us in a whimsical vortex.

Yet I knew we were on the right track. Each time we passed an emblem, I felt a surge of energy that propelled us onward.

Suddenly, the path opened before us to reveal a large, paved circular sanctuary hidden within the maze. A miniature reproduction of the maze stood in the centre of the sanctuary, with stone benches arrayed around it like the points of a compass.

"This is it, I feel it," I said, my voice barely above a whisper. "The heart of the maze. The source of its magic. We made it!"

We all cheered and looked around. A ring of tall trees stood guard around the clearing, their branches interlocking to form an al-most cathedral-like canopy. Adam spotted a carved stone on the ground with a quirky inscription.

"*Pause right here and take a break, listen to the maze, make no mistake. Hear the echoes from the past, step where they stepped, and hold fast!*" he read aloud.

"It's like the maze is talking to us!
It wants us to listen and follow," I mused,
intrigued by the playful words. Olly's tail
wagged excitedly.

Soon, words began to echo in my head,
"With courage in your paws and a wag in
your stride, sniff out where the echoes hide.
Dig where they dug, and see what you find,
maybe treasures of the very
best kind!"

I tilted my head, listening to it over
and over in my head. The words seemed
to dance in front of my eyes, urging me
to delve deeper into their meaning.

The past, present, future...
Echoes of time itself...

I closed my eyes, letting the words sink in.
And that's when it hit me. The footsteps
weren't just metaphorical they were literal!
I thought about the many paws and feet that
had trodden this ground over centuries.
"Guys, what if 'follow in their footsteps'

means to search right here, where countless others have walked?"

Adam looked at me, his eyes lighting up. "Yes, I see it now. To go where their foot-steps were! Truffle, dig here." He pointed to the oldest- looking patch of the path. "There must be something buried there."

I nodded eagerly. "Exactly! The past visitors of this maze, they've all walked here. Right in this spot. Maybe they left something behind? A clue … or maybe even the artefact itself!"

I started to dig without waiting for a reply. My paws moved swiftly, fuelled by the rush of discovery. "Come on, guys! Let's find it!" I barked excitedly.

Adam joined in, using his little hands to move the dirt. "We're real treasure hunters, aren't we, Truffle?" he grinned.

Olly, digging alongside us, chuckled. "And I'm the muscle of the operation.

Watch out for flying dirt!"

As clumps of earth flew around us, the sense of history, of countless stories buried beneath our paws, filled me. We were a part of the maze's story now, and every scoop of dirt we shovelled brought us closer to uncovering its secrets.

My heart pounded with the thrill of the hunt and anticipation of what we might find. "My canine mom would be so proud," I thought to myself.

Suddenly, there it was, nestled amid a cushion of enchanted moss. Our prize. The treasure chest.

"Wow," we all gasped together.

"How do we open it?" Olly muttered. "Oh no. It looks like we need a key."

I sighed in annoyance.

"Wait! I have an idea." Adam took off his shoe and pulled something out.

"Remember the key we found the other day? Let's see if it fits."

Adam inserted the key into the chest's lock and, with a satisfying click, it opened. Inside was the golden artefact, pulsating with the magic of the maze. It shrank and expanded rhythmically, and glowed like a miniature sun. Or, to be more precise, like a *golden bone*. It beckoned us, calling out to be held. I couldn't help but wonder how tasty it might be. Lying next to the magical bone was a mystical-looking compass and a beautiful necklace with a little round gold pendant.

I took the bone, Olly took the compass, and Adam put on the necklace. As soon as I touched the artefact, quick as a flash, it shrank until it was perfectly sized to tuck under my collar, right next to my snazzy name tag!

Olly, Adam, and I exchanged a meaningful glance. We were now the paw-some

guardians of the artefacts.

"Our discovery definitely warrants a dance," I laughed, stepping and starting to dance. Olly joined in, though his moves would never make it on Dancing with the Dogs.

Adam laughed, trying to mimic Olly's awkward twirls. "You're not exactly a smooth mover, Olly, but you've got spirit!"

Just then, a deep voice rich with wisdom and age echoed through the maze, "Congratulations, brave adventurers. You have found the artefact of the maze, a relic of immense power. The artefact has chosen you as its guardians, for your friendship is stronger than any evil magic. Use it wisely, for its magic is boundless, and its secrets are deep."

We paused in our dance, struck by the gravity of the voice. "Did the maze just talk to us?" Adam whispered, his eyes wide with awe and fear.

"Yes, it did," I replied, a sense of responsibility settling over me. "And we'll honour its message. Together."

We turned and started making our way home. An uneasy sensation now filled the maze. The mysterious stranger was there, and we could feel his presence. But we felt confident as a part of the team. The maze had chosen us and, for better or worse, we were now truly part of its legend. Our adventure was far from over. It was really only just beginning.

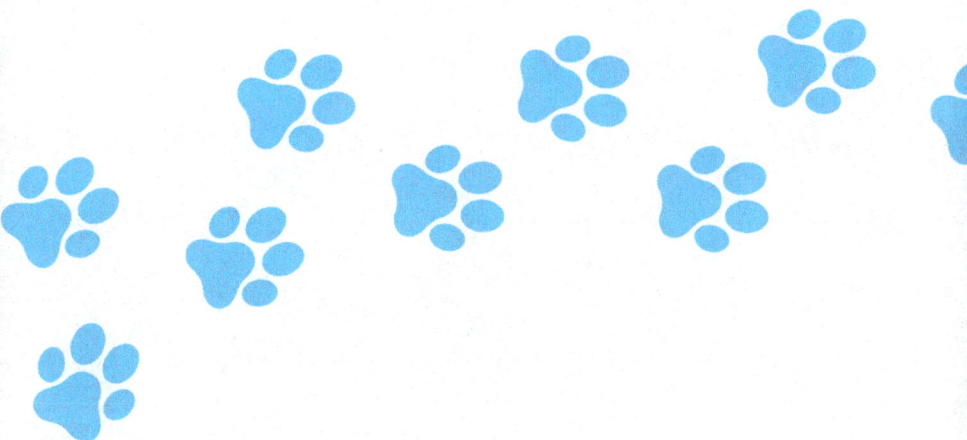

CHAPTER 5:
A HERO'S FLIGHT

The next day, to celebrate our discovery, Aga and Matt organised a picnic by the famous Rusty Laptop in Crystal Palace Park. The picnic was in full swing with animals and human friends, and laughter filled the air around us. Adam was playing with my favourite ball, and I couldn't help but feel like a proud big sister. "Nice throw, Adam!" I barked, my tail wagging with joy.

Suddenly, a cheeky duck waddled up, eyeing our snacks with unmistakable interest.

"Hey! No quacking near the crackers!" I joked, leaping into action and barking playfully as I chased it a few steps away.

"Leave some for us, ducky!" Adam laughed as he watched our little chase.

It was good fun to play picnic police, but when I looked back, Adam had disappeared. He was nowhere to be seen, and my ball lay on the ground where he had been playing.

"Adam?" I called out, my voice tinged with concern. A chill ran down my spine. The laughter and chatter around us seemed to fade into a distant hum.

"Has anyone seen a little human with a big smile and an even bigger appetite for adventure?" I asked the gathered crowd, trying to keep the mood light despite my worry. "Adam? Adam?" I called out again, hoping he was just hiding for a game of hide-and-seek. But again, there was no response, just the rustling of leaves in the gentle breeze. Panic began to set in. I rushed back to the picnic, barking loudly to alert Aga and Matt.

"Truffle, where's Adam?" Aga's voice trembled with a mother's worst fear.

As a big sister, I felt the immense burden of responsibility. Thankfully, Olly was there, his presence reassuring me as we launched a park-wide search. Animals of all shapes and sizes heeded our call, joining the mission to find Adam.

"Go, my friends! Find him!" I cried out, overwhelmed with emotion. Park onlookers stood by, stunned by the sudden animal buzz, but there was no time for explanations.

"I'm scared, Olly," I admitted, my voice shaking.

"We'll find him, Truffle. We have each other, and we have our friends," Olly said, his confidence unshaken.

As the reality of Adam's disappearance sank in, I noticed Aga and Matt frantically scanning the park. Their faces were etched with worry. The kind of worry that only parents know.

Matt was calling Adam's name, his voice growing more desperate with each call, while Aga spoke rapidly into her phone, likely calling for help.

"*We will find him*," I thought to myself. I turned to Olly and said, "We *have* to find him."

We had started heading towards the terraces when the local ancient Egyptian Sphinx, lounging on the nearby steps, gave us a warning. "Blimey, Truffle. Your mysterious stranger and his assistant Shushu, the vexed fox, have snatched Adam! He's after the artefact. He wants to harness its wicked power!"

Olly and I exchanged a look. We were facing challenges that seemed as confusing as a cat barking or a dog meowing, but we were determined, we were united, and we were ready to do whatever it took to get Adam back.

As the sun dipped lower, the urgency ramped up. We had to locate Adam before the sun kissed the horizon goodbye.

I started sniffing the ground to find traces of Adam, running from tree to tree as fast as I could. All of a sudden, I felt the strangest sensation.

"Olly, my ears are spinning!" I shouted. With a whizz and buzz, whizz, buzz, bum... I started to feel dizzy and light.

"WOW! Truffle, you're flying!" Olly gasped, his tail wagging super fast. "That's paw-some!"

Despite my fear of heights, I took to the skies, gliding over the park like an overly enthusiastic kite.

The view from above was a carpet of emerald green woven with hidden path ways, mystical groves, and what looked suspiciously like a garden in the shape of a cat.

"Truffles, the compass! Maybe the compass can help us find Adam," Olly screamed up into the air, pulling the shiny compass they had found the day before from his bag.

"But what if we can't find him?" I was starting to worry about keeping my balance flying in the air.

"We will," Olly replied from the ground, panting to keep up with me but determined not to fall behind. "We've got all park animals on our side, remember? It's like we are all little superheroes!"

With Olly leading the way with the compass down below, we soon found ourselves by the little pond that surrounded the park's dinosaur guardians. As I flew down to the ground, we the familiar rumbling voice of Mr Megalosours, the same dinosaur who had already helped us before.

"Ah, my brave adventurers, seeking the young one snatched by the sly Shushu," the old guardian of the park's secrets intoned, his voice echoing slightly. "Follow the trail where the bluebells nod, head past where the willows weep, and journey into the fog."

His dinosaur friends, Mr and Ms Iguanodon, added, "Listen close, for each clue is a key. In Shushu's den, what you seek, you'll see. Beware the whispers that lead astray, find your friend, and save the day."

We thanked the old dinosaurs for the rhyming guidance, their words settling deep in our hearts.

"Bluebells, willows, and then the fog," Olly repeated, memorising the sequence. "Got it. Let's not get lost in the bog!" he added with forced humour.

"We need to find the bluebells. Do you know where could they be?" I asked.

Olly shook his head. With a mix of desperation and hope, he took out the compass and whispered, "Bluebells." Suddenly, the little gold arrow sprang to life, pointing the way. We exchanged amazed glances. This compass was more than it seemed.

We followed the arrow until we reached a thicket of bluebells. Each step felt like peeling back a layer of a hidden puzzle, one that held the key to finding Adam. The bluebells soon led us to a willow grove, their branches swaying like arrows ushering us forward.

"Next, 'head past where the willows weep'," I repeated, feeling the tension build.

Olly whispered to the compass and again the arrow shifted, now pointing deeper into the park. My heart pounded as willow trees thickened around us, their branches swirling like ghostly tendrils. Following the rhyme felt like walking on a tightrope between hope and fear. Every rustle of leaves made us jump.

We continued onwards, each step bringing us closer to Adam and the unknown dangers lurking ahead, driven by the urgency to save Adam.

"We're coming, Adam," I whispered into the wind, hoping that somewhere, somehow, he could hear us.

A fog appeared around our feet and grew denser with every step. Soon the path ahead became barely visible, hiding our footsteps, but the compass arrow remained a steady beacon in the uncertainty.

The air grew thick with tension. We knew the final destination was near, but the thick fog hid any sign of where we were going, or how far we had to go. Our breaths quickened, the silence between us filled with unspoken fears and unwavering determination.

"Hold on, Truffle," Olly whispered, his voice trembling yet firm. "We're almost there."

Finally, the dense fog cleared and we found ourselves standing outside the entrance to a cave. The entrance was cloaked in tangled vines, disguising a dark passage that led deep into the earth. We exchanged a determined glance and cautiously stepped inside, following the passage until it opened into a large, open den.

The den was dimly lit. The only light filtered in through cracks in the stone ceiling overhead casting ghostly patterns on the walls. In the centre of the underground chamber stood a tall, red-coated fox with a bushy tail, small eyes, and big teeth. "That must be Shushu!" Olly whispered.

Shushu, I must say, looked rather scary.

Shushu stood there waiting for them, his bright red fur aglow and a stinky smirk stretched across his lips. His lair was a chaotic collection of stolen trinkets and mysterious objects, but our attention was fixed on one thing only: Adam. He was standing in a large basket, his eyes wide with a mix of fear and brave defiance. And, somehow, he was wearing a pilot's hat.

"I'm not afraid of you, Shushu!" Adam declared, his voice surprisingly steady. He had fashioned a small tool from a stick and a piece of string he'd found in his pocket, and was trying to untie the knot that held the basket closed.

It was clear that Adam wasn't just waiting to be rescued. He was actively trying to find a way out himself.

Shushu turned to greet us. "Oh, my dear pups, you think you can outfox me, do you?" he said, his voice a menacing hiss. "I see you've brought me the artefact I've been looking for."

My heart pounded in my chest. I swallowed hard. "Let Adam go, Shushu.

Take the artefact, but please, let him go."

Olly growled beside me, his body tense and ready to spring into action at any moment. But I knew what I had to do. With a heavy heart, I carefully removed the glowing bone from my collar and held it out. The artefact pulsed with light as if protesting its handover to the nefarious fox.

Shushu's eyes gleamed with triumph. He stepped forward, his paws reaching for the artefact. "Finally," he murmured, "the power to take control of the park, London … and beyond."

"Adam, run!" I yelled.

Just as Adam started to climb out of the basket, Shushu unleashed a spell of dark magic. Several enchanted air balloons instantly materialised. One of them swiftly attached itself to Adam's basket and before we could react, began to lift him and the basket into the air.

With another wave of magic, the earth began to rumble and tremble. The earth split open overhead and a shaft of light pierced through the darkness of the underground den. Dust and debris fell down on them as the den's ceiling opened up like a trapdoor to the sky. The walls fell away revealing more and more of the dusky sky with each passing second.

The air balloon continued to ascend with Adam still in it. The basket swayed from side to side as it rose toward the new gap overhead. Adam's silhouette became smaller and smaller as the basket drifted up out of the open roof of the den and into the sky beyond. Olly and I could only watch as he finally disappeared into the vast expanse of the evening sky.

"Adam!" I barked, my voice filled with desperation. The sight of him drifting away filled us with a renewed sense of urgency. We had to act fast to bring him back before it was too late.

CHAPTER 6:

DANCING IN THE AIR

"You're too late to stop my grand plan. Thank you for the artefact but you must go now," Shushu laughed, his voice sharp and mean.

I felt a surge of fear and anger. "Don't underestimate me, Shushu! Friendship is stronger than any trick you have!" I screamed. Panic and desperation gripped me. This wasn't how it was supposed to happen. "Adam!" I barked, my voice echoing off the den walls.

Olly growled, his stance ready for a fight. "Fly to get Adam, Truffle!" he urged. "It's our only chance!"

"I can't," I gasped in sadness. "I don't have the magical artefact anymore."

Olly, giving Truffle his widest smile and an encouraging tone, squeaked, "It was never the golden bone that gave you magic. The magic was always within you. Believe in yourself. Fly!"

Putting my trust in Olly's words, I leapt into action with newfound determination and concentrated as hard as I could. All of a sudden, I felt my ears unfurl and my paws lift off the ground. At first, I wobbled and flailed as I tried to find my balance in the air. I gradually adjusted to this new way of moving and managed to steady myself.

My ears caught the wind and I soared upward, chasing after Adam and the hot air balloon. My heart pounded with fear and confidence, each flap of my ears lifting me higher and filling me with the belief that I could do this.

Down below, Olly engaged Shushu in a whirlwind of paws and tails, the blur of his actions focused on keeping the sly fox from interfering.

I focused my sights on Adam, whose pilot hat was now rather fitting for the circumstances. He looked down and saw me. *"Oh, crumbs! I must rescue him, and I must do it now!"* I thought, the sight of him fuelling my resolve. I looked around desperately for a way to help him.

All of a sudden I heard a cry from below. I looked down to see Swan Sam flying towards me. *"Perfect timing,"* *I thought. "Sam will know just what to do!"*

Sam was a local swan from the park and he had a reputation for his graceful flying skills.

With a sense of urgency tickling my paws, I turned to Swan Sam and cried, "Sam, old bird, it's time for a soaring rescue!"

"Don't you worry, Truffle. Let's soar to new heights! Follow me," Swan Sam called, his majestic wings flapping ever faster. I felt my own newfound flying powers begin to pulse within me. The wind under my wings and ears felt exhilarating!

We zoomed upwards dodging wayward kites and startling a flock of rather grumpy pigeons. Sam swerved gracefully around a cloud while I used all my strength to create a gust of wind that propelled me straight through the white nimbus.

"Steady on, Truffle!" Swan Sam called over the rush of air. "We're approaching the basket!"

My heart pounded as we came alongside Adam's airborne prison. He looked at us, eyes wide and filled with hope. "Hold on, Adam!" I barked.

The balloon bobbed and weaved in the wind, making the journey bumpy, but my determination was unwavering. I was so close now. Close enough to see the fear and hope in Adam's eyes.

Swan Sam skilfully matched the basket's speed and managed to keep it balanced while I leapt over the edge and into the basket. Once inside, I quickly scratched a small hole in the enchanted balloon to slowly release the air trapped inside. Soon, our rapid ascent slowed until we started to gently descend back down to the ground.

Adam hugged me tightly and cheered, "I knew you'd come! I love you, my sister."

At that moment I felt so, so happy.

The park below swirled with activity. Animals of all kinds had gathered, their faces turned upwards, watching our descent with held breath. The wind slowly guided us back to the safety of the earth. Back to where our friends and family waited.

We landed with a gentle thud amidst cheers and cries of relief. Aga and Matt rushed forward and enveloped Adam and I in a tight embrace. Olly trotted over with a triumphant grin on his face. Shushu was nowhere in sight.

"You did it, Truffle!" Olly exclaimed. "You saved him!"

"See, I told you we'd get him back," I woofed, unable to hide my happiness. "They say cats have nine lives. Well, they can start saying that dogs have ear-wings!"

Swan Sam chuckled heartily, "Indeed, Truffle. It seems you've got more than flappy ears. You've got flappy wings! And ears of courage!"

"You're a hero, Truffle!" everyone cheered.

"Thank you, Truffle," Aga exclaimed, hugging me as if I'd just won an Olympic gold medal.

"You've done something extraordinary. You are a hero, our super-trouper-Truffle," Matt added, his voice heavy with emotion.

I nuzzled Adam gently, feeling a swell of pride. "You were incredibly brave, Adam," I said.

"Thanks for coming for me, Truffle," Adam reached over and wrapped his arms tightly around me.

"We're a team, Adam. We'll always look out for each other."

Adam's grip relaxed as he pulled back, a brave smile breaking through. "I love you, Truffle. You're the best big sister a brother could ask for.'

At that moment, our bond felt stronger than ever.

"Come on, everyone! Let's celebrate. There's cake and drinks, and all the best park games!" Matt called out, interrupting our embrace.

"A party for me?" I wagged my tail.

"No, Truffle, a party for all of us! For teamwork, friendship, and bravery!" Olly explained.

"Everyone played a part!" Adam said with a grin.

The park burst into life around us. The bees were buzzing and the birds were chirping. For a few moments, everyone forgot about being an animal or a bug or

a human. We were all just friends celebrating.

Adam tugged at my fur gently, his eyes twinkling like the stars. "Truffle," he whispered, grinning. "Can we go explore some more tomorrow?"

I laughed, "Of course! We need to finish discovering everything for your guide-book!"

★ ★ ★

Later that evening as everyone danced and sang around us, our little pack gathered to discuss an important matter. "Let's set out on another quest tomorrow," Adam suggested.

"We need to find Shushu and stop him before he uses the magical bone to cook up some evil," Olly spoke up.

"I agree. We must intervene," I added, nodding firmly.

"Don't you know?" A voice announced behind us. We looked around and saw the Egyptian Sphinx, who had come to our aid rescuing Adam, had joined the conversation.

"Shushu cannot wield the artefact's powers without the necklace that Adam is wearing and the compass that Olly is carrying."

We looked at each other and a wave of relief washed over us.

"That's fantastic news!" exclaimed Adam, his face lighting up with hope and excitement.

However, the Sphinx's next words tempered our jubilation.

"But be wary, young adventurers. You must recover the magic bone swiftly. If Shushu is working with the mysterious stranger and they discover how to override

the necklace's protection, who knows what they would use its power for."

Adam, Olly and I exchanged determined glances. The mix of relief was now fused with a newfound urgency.

Later that night, we headed home as night descended on the park. Our hearts were full of resolve and our paws (and little hands!) ready to spring into action.

After a hearty meal of schnitzel and warm pierogi, I snuggled into bed beside Adam and reflected on our new mission. Tomorrow, we will embark on a new adventure. Not just any adventure, but a crucial mission to safeguard the park.

"Goodnight, Truffle," Adam yawned.

"Goodnight, Adam," I whispered back, hearing his heavy breathing as he fell into a deep sleep. I rolled over and laid my head down to sleep, but sleep escaped me as thoughts filled my head.

Love and friends can achieve anything when they believe in themselves.
Magic may have shown me the way, but it was my friendship with Olly, Adam, Sam Swan, and all the animals of the park that had saved the day. The warmth of my family's embrace and the joy in Adam's eyes filled my heart with contentment.

But something kept nagging at my thoughts. An uncomfortable feeling, like a hyperactive frog hopping around my brain: the artefact was still out there, and it was now in the cunning paws of sly Shushu the fox.

And I knew that the magic artefact wasn't just a useless trinket. It had power. *Immense* power.

And I secretly believed in my heart that it held the power to help me find my long-lost siblings, Peanut, Coco, Buli, and Oreo.

I knew deep in my heart that the adventure wasn't over.

It was only just the beginning.

To Be Continued...

NEXT IN THE SERIES

Wags & Whimsy Part 2 - Adam and Truffle Save London

AUTHOR

Agnieszka Gradzewicz-Akal

Hi

Born in Poland and now living in the United Kingdom, Agnieszka first found her passion for storytelling as a child writing enchanted tales of forest sprites and wise storks. Despite the dance of dyslexia that scrambled letters on her pages, she never let it dim her creative spirit.

Her writing journey began in earnest during her maternity leave after finding inspiration in the enchanting Crystal Palace Park right at her doorstep. Surrounded by its historical echoes and natural beauty, Agnieszka spun her imagination into stories that blend the mystique of Polish folklore with the quaint charm of her British surroundings.

INSPIRATION

EXPLORE MORE WWW.TRUFFLEANDADAM.COM

Printed in Dunstable, United Kingdom